in the news™

FAILED STATES

Unstable Countries in the 21st Century

Matthew Bukovac

ROSEN PUBLISHING®

New York

To Mom, Dad, Kelly, and Claire, whose undying dedication to humanitarian efforts was a constant inspiration for this book

Published in 2011 by The Rosen Publishing Group, Inc.
29 East 21st Street, New York, NY 10010

Copyright © 2011 by The Rosen Publishing Group, Inc.

First Edition

Library of Congress Cataloging-in-Publication Data

Bukovac, Matthew.
Failed states : unstable countries in the 21st century / Matthew Bukovac.
    p. cm. — (In the news)
Includes bibliographical references and index.
ISBN 978-1-4358-9447-1 (library binding) —
ISBN 978-1-4488-1679-8 (pbk.) —
ISBN 978-1-4488-1687-3 (6-pack)
1. Failed states. I. Title.
JC328.7.B85 2011
320.9—dc22

                                                          2009045686

Manufactured in the United States of America

CPSIA Compliance Information: Batch #S10YA: For further information, contact Rosen Publishing, New York, New York, at 1-800-237-9932.

On the cover: Clockwise from top left: People carry sacks of grain in Somalia in 1993; the executive director of the UN World Food Programme, Josette Sheeran, is seen here in Egypt in 2009; in Batagram, Pakistan, a family explores the remains of their home, which was destroyed by the massive earthquake that hit the region in 2005.

contents

What Is a Failed State?

Off the coast of Somalia, pirates raid passing cargo ships. North Korea works on building a nuclear weapons program in violation of international law. In northern Pakistan, ongoing military engagements with the Taliban displace millions from their homes. Five million children live as orphans in the war-ravaged streets of Iraq, as armed militant groups fight with each other. These events are taking place in countries that have come to be known as failed states. Failed states are countries where the government has failed at its basic responsibilities.

There are many reasons why states fail. Sometimes natural disasters, such as earthquakes, devastate a country, leaving its infrastructure ruined and the government unable to help those affected by the disaster. Sometimes wars and political struggles cause states to fail. Sometimes a nation's government does not have control over the territory of the country or is unable to provide basic living conditions for its citizens. According to Ashraf Ghani and Claire Lockhart, authors of the book *Fixing Failed States*, more than a billion people, in over forty nations, live in failed states.

People living in failed states are often impoverished. When the government of a failed state is weak or nonexistent, it often cannot effectively fight crime

These Sunni Iraqis live in a refugee camp in Kurdish Iraq. Refugees in this camp survive by begging, and the majority of children are unable to attend school.

FAILED STATES INDEX 2009

| Alert | Warning | Moderate | Sustainable |

This map of failed states is from the Web site of the Fund for Peace (http://www.fundforpeace.org/web/). The organization collects data once a year in order to create the Failed States Index. The Failed States Index is a list of each nation and its corresponding Conflict Assessment System Tool (CAST) score.

within the country's borders. This results in an environment that is prime for illegal drug manufacturers, terrorists, and any other group that thrives in a lawless environment. Failed states can be harmful not only for the people living within their borders, but also for the entire global community.

However, not all failed states have failed governments. In contrast, stable countries that deny their citizens basic human rights, or are unwilling to peacefully interact with the world community, can also be defined as failed states.

Defining a State as Failed

In 1996, Dr. Pauline H. Baker, president of the Fund for Peace, created a system geared at defining failed states. Founded in 1957, the Fund for Peace is an independent research organization based in Washington, D.C. The organization is dedicated to promoting lasting peace and works to identify the causes of world conflict.

Baker's system for defining failed states is called the Conflict Assessment System Tool (CAST). In 2009, the Fund for Peace used CAST to assess 177 countries. All of the countries assessed by the Fund for Peace are members of the United Nations (UN). CAST uses software to review hundreds of thousands of public articles and reports relating to the political, economic, and social conditions of each country.

The Fund for Peace collects this data once per year. At the end of the collection period, experts review the data. The Fund for Peace gives each state a score based on its assessment of CAST's findings. Nations that receive a score between 90 and 120 are deemed failed states.

Since 2005, the Fund for Peace has published a yearly Failed States Index. The Failed States Index is a list of each nation reviewed by CAST and its corresponding score. In 2009, thirty-eight nations were defined as failed states and placed in the Alert Zone, the section of the index reserved for states with the highest scores. The United Nations considers this index the definitive list of failed states.

Failed States in the Media

Although dozens of countries are listed on the Failed States Index each year—typically a number somewhere in the mid-thirties—only a small number receive media attention. Failed states often receive media attention when their problems spread outside their borders, directly affecting the international community. For instance, the failed state of Iraq frequently makes headlines because of the ongoing military conflicts there. Somalia is a failed state that has been a source of recent news due to an increase in acts of piracy off its coast. Pakistan is often in the news because of its government's inability to effectively combat the terrorists that use the country as a refuge. Another failed state, North Korea, became the subject of media attention in 2003 when it withdrew from the UN Nuclear Non-Proliferation Treaty (NPT). Nearly every sovereign nation on Earth has signed the NPT, which is aimed at limiting the production and spread of nuclear weapons. Media attention

These sacks of rice are being sent to North Korea, a country that has experienced chronic food shortages and famines. North Korea is dependent on international food aid to feed its citizens.

intensified in 2006 when North Korea announced it had tested its first nuclear weapon.

No matter what failed state is being actively discussed in the news, all failed states are significant. The substantial size of the world's population living in failed states makes the issue impossible to ignore.

The following chapters will examine several failed states that are currently the focus of media scrutiny, former failed states that have managed to improve their situations, and countries that have the potential to become failed states. International efforts aimed at fixing failed states will be discussed as well.

How States Fail

2

As the Fund for Peace has aptly stated: "Each failed state fails in its own way." The countries profiled in this chapter have failed for a number of reasons. Iraq has been destabilized by wars, internal conflicts, and many years of brutal dictatorial rule. Somalia has also suffered from internal struggles and has been without a stable government since 1991. A series of government coups and political turmoil has weakened Pakistan's government, leaving it too weak to deal with the country's major problems. North Korea's government has been in place for decades, but it actively denies North Korean citizens their basic rights and is unable to provide them with the basic necessities they need to survive. Although these four countries are very different from one another, they all became classified as failed states. By taking a closer look at these countries, we can begin to understand how nations can fall into chaos.

In the town of Fallujah, Iraq, a demonstration against the U.S. military draws a crowd of thousands. The demonstrators are holding pictures of the radical Muslim cleric Moqtada al-Sadr.

Iraq

Iraq is one of the world's most infamous failed states. The country has experienced economic crises, the brutal rule of Saddam Hussein (1937–2006), and several wars fought on its soil. The Iraq War, which began in 2003, resulted in the toppling of the Hussein government, but it also left the country in a state of instability. Fighting between Sunni and Shia Muslims has created major obstacles in the process of establishing a functional government. In the midst of this chaos, vast sections of the population live as refugees.

Iraq has not always been such an unstable country. In fact, it is the site of some of humanity's greatest accomplishments. The first known civilization, Sumeria, originated prior to 5000 BCE out of the Tigris-Euphrates river valley, located in southern Iraq. Some of the earliest examples of literature, science, philosophy, and math developed in this region.

The Rule of Saddam Hussein

The story of Iraq's current troubles begins with its former leader Saddam Hussein. Hussein became president of Iraq in 1979, forcing the then current leader, Ahmed al-Bakr (1914–1982), to resign. Immediately after taking power, Hussein executed his political rivals, setting the tone of cruelty and totalitarianism that would define his twenty-four years as president.

Iraq is an especially unique failed state. During Hussein's reign, Iraq's human rights record placed it in severe violation of international law. Hussein ruthlessly cracked down on political dissent, and Iraqi citizens could be imprisoned, tortured, and even executed for speaking out against the government. Hussein also enacted a campaign of violence, known as the al-Anfal Campaign, against Iraq's minority Kurdish population. The al-Anfal Campaign lasted from 1986 until 1989. Kurdish villages were destroyed by Iraqi troops, and thousands of Kurds were killed or forcibly relocated.

Hussein used chemical weapons, considered by the UN to be weapons of mass destruction (WMDs), during the fighting. Much of this fighting took place during the Iran-Iraq War (1980–1988). Hussein also used chemical weapons against Iran. It is estimated that about five hundred thousand people were killed during the war. According to the Human Rights Watch, an independent nongovernmental organization (NGO) located in New York City, Hussein's al-Anfal Campaign resulted in the death of between fifty thousand and one hundred thousand Kurdish civilians in northern Iraq.

After Iraq's long and brutal war with Iran, Hussein entered into direct conflict with the United States in 1990 by invading the neighboring nation of Kuwait. An alliance of countries, including the United States, was opposed to this invasion and launched a UN-approved military intervention that became known as the Gulf War. This conflict lasted less than a year and ended with Iraq's defeat. The allied forces reached a cease-fire agreement with Iraq on February 28, 1991. On March 2, Saddam Hussein began the slaughter of Shia who were rebelling in the south and Kurds who were rebelling in the north.

In 2003, the United States, suspecting Iraq of being in possession of WMDs, invaded it again. This time the United States removed Hussein from power and placed him on trial for crimes against humanity. Hussein was found guilty and executed in 2006.

Iraqi resistance fighters gather to celebrate the withdrawal of U.S. troops from the city of Fallujah in 2004. Fallujah has seen a great deal of conflict during the Iraq War.

Chaos in Iraq

Since 2003 and the removal of Hussein, the former dictator's ruthless injustice has been replaced by violent chaos. A diverse group of anti–U.S. militants, called insurgents, has risen up to fight for control of the country. According to the Fund for Peace, the Iraq War, occupation, and subsequent insurgency has resulted in the displacement of more than two million people. Thirty-five percent of Iraq's children are orphans.

Fighting between Shia and Sunni Muslims has greatly added to this problem. Shia Muslims, who make up 65 percent of the nation's population, supported the move toward democracy proposed in the 2005 Iraqi constitution. Sunni Muslims, who held a favored position in Hussein's government, refused to agree to the new constitution. Violence has occurred between the two groups ever since.

Iraq's population began fleeing the country as a result of this widespread violence. This mass exodus has brought about what is referred to as a "brain drain." "Brain drain" is a term used to describe the effect that takes place in a country when its smartest and most skilled citizens leave for somewhere else. Many Iraqi intellectuals have fled the country because of the persistent violence. Seventy percent of the nation's doctors have fled, the majority settling in the neighboring nation of Jordan.

An increase in stability and security has motivated some exiled Iraqis to return to their country, but divisions between Shias and Sunnis still persist. In February 2009, U.S. president Barack Obama declared that one hundred thousand U.S. troops would leave Iraq in the summer of 2010. The future of the country is uncertain. Home to vast natural oil resources, Iraq has the potential to be one of the richest countries in Middle East. However, it must first rebuild its shattered government and economy. Peace must also be achieved between Sunnis and Shias. Many fear that this will be difficult after so many years of conflict.

In April 2009, a Kenyan soldier guards a suspected Somali pirate. He was one of eleven suspected pirates captured by an antipiracy naval mission organized by the European Union.

Somalia

Somalia has not had a stable government since 1991. Different religious, ethnic, and political groups engage in almost constant military conflict with each other. In the midst of this violence, Somalia has become home to terrible human rights violations and international crime. In 2009, Somalia ranked first in the Failed States Index.

Somalia is a country with a rich history. However, beginning in the late nineteenth century, European powers began colonizing Africa. Prior to its colonization in 1920, Somalia was an important regional power in Africa. In fact, Somalia was so strong that it held the longest-lasting anticolonial campaign against the British in history. In 1960, Somalia gained its independence and established a representative democracy. This democracy

was difficult to maintain due to fighting between different tribes. This instability allowed General Mohamed Siad Barre (1919–1995) to seize power. In 1970, Barre established a socialist military dictatorship in Somalia.

Violence on the Rise

In 1991, rival factions toppled the central government of Barre, who, fearing for his life, fled the country. After removing Barre from power, these groups began fighting with each other. The violence grew so

In 1989, a militiaman aims his rifle at a shattered portrait of Somali dictator Mohamed Siad Barre. In 1991, Barre was deposed and his regime destroyed.

bad that the UN started a humanitarian mission in Somalia in 1992. The humanitarian mission provided Somalis with food and medical aid.

In 1993, eighteen U.S. soldiers were killed in the capital city of Mogadishu. The death of these soldiers caused the UN to change the nature of its presence in the area by allowing troops on the ground to act defensively, as opposed to merely providing food and medical aide. The UN operation became a peacekeeping mission. The majority of U.S. troops involved in this mission left Somalia in 1993, and the UN peacekeeping operation ended in 1995.

Since the overthrow of Barre in 1991, no central government has been established in Somalia. Without a central government, the nation has no military or police force to prevent its citizens from breaking local and international laws. Piracy has increased off the coast of Somalia, with Somali pirates commandeering ships and often kidnapping the ships' crews. Somalia is also powerless to stop the vast human rights violations carried out by Islamic militant groups such as al-Shabaab.

Lawlessness and Piracy

Piracy began in Somalia as early as 1990. During Barre's rule, Somalia received international aid geared at developing a fishing industry. However, mass poverty and a lack of a central government meant that

Somalia was unable to prevent fishermen from other countries from using up its fishing resource. Deprived of a way to make a living, many Somali fishermen turned to piracy.

Piracy is a profitable enterprise. Somali pirates seize ships and hold the crew and cargo for ransom. Since these ransoms are typically paid, local warlords have begun funding many Somali pirates as a way to make money.

Although piracy has been taking place off the coast of Somalia since the 1990s, piracy in this region gained serious media attention with the 2009 hijacking of the *Maersk Alabama*, a U.S. container ship. This attack was the first pirate hijacking of a U.S. merchant ship since 1815. The ship's captain, Richard Phillips, allowed himself to be taken by the pirates in order to ensure his crew's safety.

The U.S. Navy attempted to negotiate for Captain Phillips's release, but the negotiations went bad after the pirates fired several shots at a small U.S. Navy boat. After the shots were fired, SEAL Team Six, an elite unit of the Navy SEALs, was deployed to free Phillips. Three of the SEAL team's snipers fired simultaneous shots, killing three of the pirates holding Phillips hostage. A fourth pirate surrendered, and Phillips was promptly rescued.

Human Rights Violations

Along with piracy, the human rights violations that occur in Somalia are also a major issue. One of the greatest perpetrators of human rights violations is the Somali Islamic extremist group al-Shabaab. In May 2009, al-Shabaab took over Mogadishu, killing hundreds in the process. Al-Shabaab instates an extreme interpretation of Sharia, the Islamic legal system, in the areas it controls. Many of the laws instated are foreign to the people in the regions conquered by al-Shabaab. For instance, all women are forced to wear burqas, an outer garment that covers the body from head to toe. Harsh punishment, such as the amputation of a limb for theft, and stoning for those found guilty of adultery, are proscribed under this legal system. The *New York Times* reported in August 2009 that al-Shabaab went as far as removing gold and silver teeth from residents in the costal town of Marka, located in the south of Somalia. Al-Shabaab considers gold and silver teeth to be overly decorative and therefore a violation of Islamic law.

Despite many attempts to correct the problems in Somalia, efforts have yielded little success. The recent increase in piracy has created unprecedented unity in the international community. Countries typically hostile to each other, such as Pakistan and India, have agreed to send naval ships to combat the Somali pirates. It is difficult to predict whether these efforts will be beneficial. Foreign militaries have attempted to create stability in Somalia in previous years. The most recent, Ethiopia, withdrew its peacekeeping troops in January 2009. Making matters worse, as the Fund for Peace has noted, Somalia is so incredibly dangerous, few organizations offering nonmilitary international assistance will even agree to enter the country.

Pakistan

Several factors have lead to Pakistan becoming a failed state. After decades of coups and interfighting, Pakistan's government has become weak and fractured. Because the government is so weak, it is incapable of dealing with Pakistan's greatest problems, such as attacks by the Taliban in the northern regions of the country. The government is also unable to adequately care for Pakistan's sizable refugee population, which consists of people who have fled conflicts with the Taliban and people who were displaced from their homes by earthquakes.

Pakistan was originally part of British-controlled India. After many years of struggle, India gained its independence from Britain in 1947. India is primarily a Hindu country, and the Muslim majority population of what

The city of Balakot is located in Pakistan's North-West Frontier Province. This man walks through the ruins of the city in 2005, days after it was destroyed by a massive earthquake.

would become Pakistan wanted its own state. The north-western provinces of West Punjab and Sindh became the independent nation of Pakistan.

Political Turmoil

In 1956, Pakistan experienced its first coup when General Ayub Khan overthrew the nation's young democratic government. Democratic rule returned in 1972, but lasted only until 1977, when General Muhammad Zia-ul-Haq

(1924–1988) took power in a coup. Zia-ul-Haq was responsible for officially making Pakistan an Islamic state, as well as instituting the Sharia legal code.

After Zia-ul-Haq died in a 1988 plane crash, his daughter, Benazir Bhutto (1953–2007), was elected prime minister. After being charged with corruption, Bhutto was removed from office. Reelected in 1993, She was removed once again on similar charges. In 2007, Bhutto ran a third time and was assassinated. Her husband, Asif Ali Zardari, is now president of the country.

Amid this political turmoil, Pakistan has been engaged in an ongoing armed conflict with the Taliban in its North-West Frontier Province since 2004. According to the Fund for Peace, the authority of Pakistan's government is barely recognized in this province. Local Taliban militias exercise almost total control of the area.

The Taliban

As part of the "war on terror," the United States began using drone planes to strike at Taliban targets in Pakistan as early as 2004. A drone plane is an unmanned aerial vehicle. The *London Times* reported in April 2009 that the Taliban had moved within 60 miles (97 kilometers) of Pakistan's capital of Islamabad. As a result, the United States threatened to increase its involvement in Pakistan. Pakistan has nuclear weapons, and many are afraid that they could fall into the hands of a terrorist organization.

Earthquakes and Refugees

In 2005, an earthquake (thought to be the fourteenth-most destructive earthquake in history) devastated Pakistan's North-West Frontier Province. The earthquake killed eighty thousand people and displaced more than three million from their homes. The Pakistani government was incapable of providing suitable aid to the victims of this earthquake. This left Pakistan with a large internal refugee population. Another earthquake in 2008 created even more refugees. In 2009, the government's offensive against the Taliban also displaced many people from their homes. Although some of these refugess have been resettled, the majority have not.

North Korea

North Korea's totalitarian government is considered to be one of the worst in the world. The government of North Korea is an oppressive dictatorship, headed by a man named Kim Jong II. The Fund for Peace provides an excellent description of North Korea's leadership: "The leadership of Kim Jong II is one of oppression and dysfunction and rests solely on the combination of almost religious worship of the leader and his father, Kim II Sung, and ruthless crackdowns on dissent." The government's terrible human rights record is one of the

Carrying signs and banners, approximately one million North Koreans gather in Kim II Sung Square in January 2003. They have come to hear political leaders praise Kim Jong II's decision to withdraw North Korea from the Nuclear Non-Proliferation Treaty.

main reasons why North Korea is considered to be a failed state.

Prior to World War II (1939–1945), Korea was a Japanese colony. North Korea was divided from South Korea at the end of World War II. The United States took administrative responsibilities over South Korea, and the Soviet Union took control of the North. In 1950, North Korea attacked South Korea, attempting to unify the nation. An armistice was agreed upon in 1953. An armistice is not a peace treaty; instead, it is merely an agreement to stop fighting. Technically, North Korea and South Korea have been at war for more than half a century.

A Totalitarian Government

North Korea's totalitarian government is guilty of numerous human rights violations. Kim Jong Il has ruled the country since the death of his father, Kim Il Sung, in 1994. Kim Jong Il rules North Korea absolutely, and no one can openly question his authority without running the risk of imprisonment or worse. The country lacks any democratic institutions. North Korea has no free media, freedom of religion, or independent labor unions. There is nothing to stop the state from perpetuating terrible crimes against its citizens. North Koreans have no rights, and few are allowed to leave the country.

Promises and Threats

North Korea created concern among the international community after withdrawing from the UN Nuclear Non-Proliferation Treaty (NPT) in 2003. The NPT is an agreement to stop the spread of nuclear weapons that has been signed by nearly every country in the world. The international community attempted to reach an understanding with North Korea through a series of meetings known as the Six-Party Talks. During the Six-Party Talks, China, Japan, the Russian Federation, South Korea, and the United States attempted to reach a peaceful resolution with North Korea about nuclear testing. The talks went through several rounds of meetings between 2003 and 2007.

The Six-Party Talks fell apart after North Korea launched a test rocket over Japan on April 5, 2009. The rocket landed in the Pacific Ocean. The international community condemned this act, believing it to be an attempt at intimidation and a violation of international law.

In May 2009, North Korea successfully detonated a nuclear device underground. Despite worldwide condemnation, North Korea fired four missiles into the Sea of Japan on July 2, 2009. Two days later, on July 4, 2009, North Korea tested seven ballistic missiles, which were also launched into the Sea of Japan.

International Relations

On August 17, 2009, North Korea reopened its border with South Korea. The *New York Times* speculated that North Korea's decision to open its borders might have been a reaction to UN sanctions. UN sanctions are an agreement among the organization's member nations to cease trade in or out of a country. North Korea suffers from widespread famines and is dependent on international food aid to feed its citizens. If this aid were to be shut off, the country would suffer disastrous consequences.

Finding Solutions

A diverse assortment of problems plague failed states and their citizens. A program that might help one failed state might not necessarily work in another. At the same time, a solution that works in one failed state might work in others as well. Four international organizations stand out in their attempts to aid and fix failed states. The International Monetary Fund (IMF) and the World Bank, two connected but separate organizations, are two of these groups. The other two organizations are the North Atlantic Treaty Organization (NATO) and the UN.

The IMF and World Bank

The IMF works to aid in the organization of the world economy. This organization has three main functions. The first function of the IMF is to monitor financial development and attempt to prevent crises in developing and at-risk nations. The second is to lend money to

The International Monetary Fund (IMF) was founded on July 1, 1944, at the International Monetary Conference held in Bretton Woods, New Hampshire. An international organization, the IMF had 186 member countries in 2009.

nations in the hope of preventing the spread of poverty. The third function is to provide technical assistance to countries aimed at improving their economy.

The World Bank acts rather similarly to the IMF. To be a member of the World Bank, a nation must also be a member of the IMF. The World Bank is divided into two sections. The largest section is the International Bank of Reconstruction and Development (IBRD). This institution, made up of 186 member countries, focuses on middle-income and poor countries with good financial credit. The other section of the World Bank is the International Development Association (IDA). The IDA, which is comprised of 168 member nations, focuses its attention on the poorest nations in the world.

Despite these organizations' expressed goals, their efforts have yielded mixed results. Haiti, Kenya, and Jamaica are three examples of nations that these organizations have sought to develop. In each of these cases, critics have accused the IMF and World Bank of instituting practices that ensure the nations receiving aid will develop high levels of debt.

The money that the IMF and World Bank provide to struggling nations comes in the form of a loan that must be repaid. Countries that receive these loans may be incapable of doing so, leaving them dependent on these organizations. In an attempt to pay off their debt, countries may adopt new economic practices that can have negative consequences for their citizens. For example, indebted countries are encouraged to shift their farm resources from national food production to producing crops to export. By selling these crops, countries can raise money to repay their debt. However, this can result in there being less food for the indebted countries' citizens. In countries already suffering from food shortages, this can have serious consequences. Since 2006, the IMF and World

The IMF's International Monetary and Financial Committee (IMFC) meets at IMF headquarters in Washington, D.C., on April 25, 2009. The IMF provides assistance to countries in the form of a loan.

Bank have participated in reform aimed at improving their success rates and public image.

NATO and the UN

NATO and the UN have also attempted to improve the conditions in failed states. These two organizations often work together in matters of international security. NATO frequently helps the UN enforce sanctions.

NATO was created in 1949 in Brussels, Belgium. An alliance of twenty-eight member countries, the group's initial goal was to serve as a political and military alliance aimed at countering the Soviet Union and Eastern Bloc. The Eastern Bloc refers to European nations that were allied with, or indirectly controlled by, the Soviet Union. After the fall of the Soviet Union and the end of the Cold War, many of the countries in the Eastern Bloc were thrown into turmoil as they seized independence. NATO reassessed its purpose and decided to focus on helping these countries develop economically.

Since the September 11, 2001, terrorist attacks on the World Trade Center and the Pentagon, NATO has focused a good deal of its attention on the Middle East. September 11 was the first time NATO enacted Article 5 of its charter. This article states that an attack against one NATO member nation would be treated as an attack on all. In April 2003, NATO took command of the International Security Assistance Force (ISAF), a development and security operation created by the United Nations Security Council. The goal of the ISAF is to create a secure environment that will allow the country of Afghanistan to achieve a democratic state. The ISAF currently faces heavy resistance from the Taliban and participates in almost daily intensive combat.

In the northwestern Buner district in Pakistan, a displaced woman receives food from the United Nations World Food Programme. Established in 1962, the UN World Food Programme is dedicated to fighting hunger worldwide.

The UN's participation in failed states takes many forms. The UN not only deploys peacekeepers, military forces aimed at arresting conflict in warring nations, but also provides humanitarian aid. The World Food Programme, one of the larger humanitarian branches of the UN, provides more than one hundred million people with food in nations all over the globe. Another UN group aimed at providing humanitarian aid is the United Nations Children's Fund (UNICEF), which focuses on assisting mothers and children in developing nations.

Another branch of the UN involved in helping failed states is the United Nations Human Rights Council. This group monitors human rights violations across the globe. The Human Rights Council reports to the UN General Assembly about what actions should be taken to resolve an issue. The UN is also capable of imposing sanctions on countries that fail to reach certain standards of human rights or engage in aggressive behavior toward their neighbors. Sanctions are a series of restrictions that the UN places on a country. For instance, economic sanctions can restrict a country's trade. Sanctions allow the UN to exert international pressure on a country without having to resort to the use of military force.

Although no single group or organization can claim a full solution to the problems of failed states, each provides failed states with essential services and assistance. The ongoing efforts of these organizations to maintain basic levels of stability in failed states make future progress possible.

The Road to Recovery

4

I t is possible for a failed state to improve its conditions, but it can take decades for a failed state to become a functional state. Despite the fact that failed states are an international concern, the greatest seeds for change often come from within the failed state itself. Investing in national infrastructure, increased trade, and international cooperation have all proven to help failed states recover.

International Cooperation

Ireland is a nation that went from being very impoverished to being very successful. Ireland has historically suffered tremendous troubles, ranging from famine to civil war. As recently as the 1960s, Ireland was one of the poorest nations in Europe. Its gross domestic product (GDP), the total value of goods and services produced by a nation in a year, was only 60 percent of the European average. By 2007, the Irish GDP had grown to 140 percent of the European average. Ireland now provides one of the highest qualities of life in the world. China, another nation historically marked by poverty, now has the fourth-largest economy in the world. Both of these nations owe a great deal of their success to participating in the global economy.

Starting in the early 1990s, Ireland began opening its borders to foreign investment. This proved to be so successful that people referred to Ireland's rapid economic growth as the Celtic Tiger.

Many men and women make up the staff of Ireland's Dell Enterprise Command Center in 2004. Ireland's choice to develop its technological infrastructure was a major factor in its economic recovery.

China's economic growth and reform began in 1978 and occurred much more gradually. During the 1970s and 1980s, China instated economic policies that allowed for greater amounts of international trade. In 1996, China began a series of economic reforms that sought to privatize industries previously run by the government. To privatize an industry means that ownership and control is transferred from the government to private individuals or groups. In 2001, China joined the World Trade Organization (WTO), an international organization that

This billboard in the Chinese city of Beijing promotes the country's bid to join the World Trade Organization (WTO). China became a member of the WTO in 2001.

seeks to promote international trade. Soon after, China opened up its largest national bank to international investment.

Investing in Infrastructure

The word "infrastructure" is used to describe all of the buildings, roads, communication methods, and energy sources a society uses to function. Both China and Ireland improved their economies by investing heavily in their infrastructures.

In 1973, Ireland became a member of the European Communities, a trade institution that united the nations of Europe. Membership in the European Communities gave Ireland access to grants focused on developing its infrastructure. Ireland took these grants and built rail lines and highways. The country also invested money in improving city streets across the country. These developments united the nation, giving citizens, as well as businesses, easier access to the whole of the country.

The strength of China's economy is also tied to the development of its infrastructure. Since China became a Communist country in 1949, developing the nation's infrastructure has been one of the state's primary goals. China is the fourth-largest country, by land mass, in the world. It is also the world's most populous country, with approximately 1.3 billion people. China's vast territory has made the development of nationwide infrastructure a long and difficult process.

China opened its first subway system in Beijing in 1970. Ten years later, another subway line opened in the city of Tiajin. In 1986, China laid approximately 480,000 miles (772,485 km) of road. These roads created an easy and efficient way of distributing goods between cities. On average, China spends about 10 percent of its gross domestic product on infrastructure development.

India is another country that is flourishing despite many years of hardship. It is the seventh-largest nation in the world in terms of land mass, and it has a population of more than one billion people. India's large population means that its economy is inherently tied to the development of its infrastructure. In 1998, India began its National Highways Development Project. This project set out to improve India's vast highway system. As of 2006, India had spent $71 billion on highway development. In the book *Fixing Failed States*, the authors estimate that India will need to spend another $350 billion on developing and improving its infrastructure if it wishes to maintain the speed of its economic development.

Participating in a World Economy

Improving infrastructure benefits a nation in a number of ways. It grants the nation's citizens easier access to goods and their nation as a whole. It also improves the position the country has in the world economy.

Prior to developing its infrastructure, Ireland was incapable of moving products in or out of the country in a manner efficient enough to allow it to participate in trade and investment. The improvement of Ireland's infrastructure changed all this. One of the most successful economic decisions that Ireland made was to position itself as the "eHub," or center of industry related to computers and the Internet, for Europe. By 2005, after developing its infrastructure and entering into the computer market, Dell, Apple, and Hewlett Packard had opened manufacturing plants in Ireland. Microsoft's European headquarters is located in Dublin, the capital city of Ireland.

Ireland recognized that the growing technology market, combined with its geographic location between the United States and the rest of Europe, made it an attractive location to foreign computer companies. Because it had developed its infrastructure, Ireland was able to fully capitalize on its most basic strengths. This allowed the country to branch out and participate in the world economy.

India, like Ireland, realized technology could be a pillar of its economy. But unlike Ireland, India already possessed a long-standing computer industry, dating back to the 1960s. With the birth of the Internet in the

Steve Ballmer, chief executive officer of Microsoft, gives a speech at the Hyderabad International Convention Center in India in 2009. India's commitment to developing its computer and technological industries has played a major part in its economic improvement.

1990s, India instituted a series of economic reforms, as well as communication development plans, to improve the country's ability to participate in an already familiar industry. In 1998, Prime Minister Atal Bihari Vajapayee created the Indian National Task Force on Information Technology and Software Development. Today, the technology industry in India is so prominent that Hyderabad, an Indian city that serves as a major computer and communication center, has been nicknamed Cyberabad.

Privatization and Development in China

Although no one industry can be cited as the root of China's recent economic development, China's decision to allow the private ownership of its manufacturing plants has enabled the country to participate in the world economy. For many years, the Chinese government controlled all of the country's manufacturing and severly restricted private enterprise. Once China eased these restrictions, its economy began improving. According to the U.S. Consumer Product Safety Commission, the percentage of goods imported from China into the United States increased 300 percent between 1997 and 2004. The increase was a direct result of China's economic reforms. In 2007, the U.S. Consumer Product Safety Commission stated that China manufactured 40 percent of all goods imported into the United States.

China's rapid development has come under criticism by some economists. Peter Morici, who began teaching business at the University of Maryland after serving as the chief economist at the U.S. International Trade Commission, told CNN that China allows manufacturers to do "whatever they want without regulation." China's vast deregulation, while allowing it to create cheaper and therefore more profitable goods, has often resulted in the production of unsafe products. One of the most famous examples of an unsafe product imported from China was poisonous pet food that arrived in the United States in 2007. This deadly pet food contained a substance called melamine, which caused fatal kidney failure in hundreds of dogs and cats.

China's claims to safe production methods suffered another blow in 2008 when Chinese-made infant formula imported into the United States was found to be contaminated. This infant formula was also contaminated with melamine. The contaminated formula resulted in three hundred thousand infants getting sick and six infants dying. As a result of this scandal, countries around the world issued recalls of potentially unsafe food products made in China. The Chinese government has since arrested dozens of people in connection with the sale of contaminated food products. The World Health Organization (WHO), an agency of the United Nations that specializes in international public health, stated that this event was not an isolated incident, but a large-scale intentional activity geared at cutting corners to make money.

Looking to the Future

For every failed state that begins to show signs of improvement, there are others where conditions are getting worse. Whereas recovery is typically a lengthy process, the disintegration of a nation's stability can seem like it happens overnight. As illustrated earlier in this book, a variety of conditions can qualify a country to be a failed state. Once a state reaches a point of failure, the conditions its citizens are forced to live under typically decline rapidly.

Speculation on Future Failed States

One of the most common symptoms of state failure is the inability of a government to stop nongovernmental groups from using violence as a way to control others. As discussed earlier, this has been an issue in Pakistan: The Pakistani government has been unable to gain full control of Pakistan's North-West Frontier Province. This part of the country is controlled by Taliban militants who maintain their power by force. Pakistan is not the only country with this problem.

Mexico

The Mexican government has been unable to stop violent drug cartels that operate in the southern part of the country. According to the *Wall Street Journal*, "kidnappings and extortion are common" in this part of Mexico. In early 2009, the U.S. Defense Department (oftentimes referred to as the Pentagon) published a report warning that Mexico may be at risk of becoming a failed state.

In Mexico City, eight members of a drug cartel are held at the Mexico Federal Police command center in June 2009.

One of the many jobs of the Pentagon is to predict future military conflicts that could involve the United States. Mexico's ongoing war with drug cartels has become serious enough to attract the Pentagon's attention. Drug cartels are criminal organizations that focus on developing and controlling the trafficking of drugs. These organizations can range from loosely held partnerships between small drug manufacturers to highly organized criminal enterprises.

In 2009, David Shirk of the Trans-Border Institute at the University of San Diego stated at a hearing for the House Subcommittee on Commerce that six thousand civilians died in Mexico last year in cartel-related crimes. The *Los Angeles Times* reported, in August 2009, that eleven thousand people have died in Mexico's struggle against drug cartels since President Felipe Calderón, who is often given credit for beginning Mexico's war on drugs, took office in 2006.

In the midst of this violence, Mexico exhibits another symptom of state failure: a lack of government credibility. In the book *Mexico Unconquered*, John Gibler, a Global Exchange human rights delegate, explains that in Mexico, "government employees protect the most wanted criminals from the law, while at the same time carrying out a war against these criminals."

Mexico has a long history of corruption extending into almost every branch of the government. This has greatly affected Mexico's ability to effectively combat drug trafficking. For example, in 2008 Noé Ramírez Mandujano, the anti-recreational drug chief of Mexico's Specialized Investigation of Organized Crime, was arrested for accepting $450,000 a month in bribes from drug cartels.

Corruption in Mexico's police organizations has led President Calderón to allocate twenty-five thousand troops to fighting drug cartels. This decision has come under criticism from some human rights advocates such as Louise Arbour, who serves as the United Nation's high commissioner for human rights. Arbour stated on Mexican television that the decision to involve the military was "dangerous" because of the Mexican military's long history of human rights abuses.

Despite the dire statistics surrounding Mexico's ongoing war with drug cartels, many feel that the country is not on the verge of state failure. Larry Rohter, a former *New York Times* Latin American affairs correspondent, argued in an article for the paper that while Mexico may be facing problems with drug cartels, conditions in the country have improved significantly in the past decade. In his article, Rohter stated, "In contrast to the secretive, suspicious one-party state I left behind, the Mexico on view today is clearly a democracy— flawed and fractious, but up and running."

Saudi Arabia

Saudi Arabia is another country that many feel could become a failed state. The House of Saud, the monarchy that rules Saudi Arabia, is criticized for human rights violations. The House of Saud governs the country through a strict interpretation of Sharia law. Women's rights are severely restricted in the country, and people found guilty of committing a crime can face brutal corporal punishment. Saudi citizens are not allowed to criticize the government. The news media is censored, and all political parties are banned. At the same time, some fear that Islamic terrorists may overthrow the

Prince Mohammed bin Nayef survived an August 28, 2009, attack by a suicide bomber in Jeddah, Saudi Arabia. Bin Nayef is seen here in a hospital several days after the attack.

Saudi royal family, which could lead to even worse problems.

Terrorism in Saudi Arabia stretches back over a decade. The world's most famous terrorist, Osama bin Laden, is a native of Saudi Arabia, along with fifteen of the nineteen 9/11 hijackers. Beginning in 2003, Saudi Arabia has suffered a series of terrorist attacks. This led the country to attempt a swift and decisive crackdown on terrorism. Saudi Arabia succeeded at killing and capturing enough members of al Qaeda to force a large section of its membership out of the country. However, the terrorist organization moved only as far as the neighboring country of Yemen.

On August 30, 2009, al Qaeda claimed responsibility for a bombing that injured Prince Mohammed bin Nayef. Bin Nayef is a senior member of the Saudi royal family and a deputy interior minister in charge of counterterrorism. A terrorist traveled to his home and detonated a concealed bomb. This event demonstrated that the Saudi royal family was still vulnerable to attacks by Islamic militants. Despite the best efforts of the Saudi government, and the greatest hopes of the international community, Saudi Arabia is still far from solving its terrorist problem.

Thailand

Thailand is another example of a nation with uncertain state stability. Since 1932, Thailand has had seventeen different constitutions. Many transitions from one government to another have been accompanied by violence.

In 2006, the Royal Thai Army staged a coup led by General Sonthi Boonyaratglin. This junta, which is a military or political group that rules a country after taking power by force, took control of Thailand. The junta claimed that the motivation for the coup was the massive corruption and human rights violations the state was guilty of under the rule of the prime minister, Thaksin Shinawatra. The army instated martial law, arrested government cabinet members, and censored the media. Prime Minister Thaksin was put on trial, but no evidence could be found to support the accusations of corruption. Martial law was lifted after a year, as was promised by the leaders of the coup. In 2007, Thailand held elections, but only after banning Thaksin's political party, the Thai Rak Thai, from the process.

Unfortunately, this was not the end of political turmoil in Thailand. In May 2008, Samak Sundaravej, who had been elected prime minister in December 2007, was asked to resign by a political party called the People's Alliance for Democracy (PAD). They claimed that Samak was a puppet of Thaksin and began staging protests against Samak. The situation became a crisis on August 26, 2008, when protesters took over the grounds of the Government House, which is the office of the Thai prime minister. Samak was later removed from office.

Protestors clash with police during an August 29, 2008, demonstration at the Government House in Bangkok, Thailand. The protestors were demanding that Prime Minister Samak Sundaravej resign from office.

Samak's removal from office did little to quell political tension in the country. He was replaced as prime minister by Somchai Wongsawat. PAD rejected Somchai on the grounds that he was Thaksin's brother-in-law. Conflicts with Somchai reached a critical point in October 2008 when PAD besieged parliament to prevent Somchai from being able to formally announce any policies. The following month, PAD forces took over Suvarnabhuni International Airport. Although PAD eventually left the airport, violent demonstrations have continued. In April 2009, clashes between the two groups caused the government to declare a state of emergency.

To make matters worse, Thailand's government faces other problems besides instability. In 2009, Thailand experienced terrorist attacks by Islamic militants who desire their own state. Thailand also suffers from rampant drug trade and human trafficking. Many people worry that Thailand's political turmoil, violation of human rights, and inability to control both drug cartels and terrorists could result in the country becoming a failed state.

Conclusion

A prediction of a state's future failure is only that: a prediction. Mexico, Saudi Arabia, and Thailand are merely three countries among many nations that could possibly become failed states. And although the process of diagnosing state failure involves a complex analytical process, the process of fixing failed states is far less advanced. Certain practices, such as greater participation in the world economy and the development of national infrastructure, have helped some countries improve their situation. However, there are no certain solutions for failed states. What is certain is that the lives of more than a billion people, the effects of international crime, and the threats of terrorism and nuclear war are too serious to ignore.

Glossary

brain drain The emigration of a nation's brightest and most skilled citizens.

coup Abbreviation of the French phrase *coup d'etat*, which means an illegal and violent seizure of government power.

drone plane A reusable, unmanned aerial vehicle capable of controlled level flight.

eHub A location that serves as a technological center of a given area.

failed state Any nation whose government has failed at the basic responsibilities of a sovereign state.

gross domestic product (GDP) The total value of goods and services produced by a nation in a single year.

infrastructure Physical structures that are necessary for a country or society to function, such as roads, power plants, sewage systems, and public transit systems.

international law Common laws, rules, and guidelines.

martial law Military rule over a country. Martial law is instated during times of great crisis.

North Atlantic Treaty Organization (NATO) An international military alliance. NATO has twenty-six member countries located in Europe and North America.

Nuclear Non-Proliferation Treaty (NPT) An international treaty aimed at limiting the spread of nuclear weapons.

SEAL Team Six The Navy SEALs' most elite counterterrorism team.

Shia Muslims Adherents of Shia Islam, a branch of the Islamic religion that makes up approximately 10 to 15 percent of Muslims around the world. Shia Muslims made up the majority of Muslims in Iraq.

Six-Party Talks A series of negotiations that took place between the United States, the Russian Federation, the People's Republic of China, Japan, South Korea, and North Korea. The Six-Party Talks were aimed at finding a peaceful resolution to security concerns brought about by North Korea's nuclear weapons program.

sovereign The quality of self-governance. Sovereign nations are those that make their own laws and control their own resources.

Sunni Muslims Adherents of Sunni Islam, a branch of the Islamic religion. Sunni Muslims make up the majority of Muslims worldwide.

World Bank An international banking institution created to control economic aid for member nations and make loans in times of crisis.

For More Information

Amnesty International
5 Penn Plaza
New York, NY 10001
(212) 807-8400
Web site: http://www.amnesty.org
Amnesty International undertakes research and action focused on preventing and ending human rights abuses.

Fund for Peace
1720 Eye Street NW, 7th Floor
Washington, DC 20006
(202) 223-7490
Web site: http://www.fundforpeace.org
Fund for Peace is an independent research and education organization that focuses on identifying and reducing conflict stemming from weak or failed states.

UNICEF
United States Fund for UNICEF
125 Maiden Lane, 11th Floor
New York, NY 10038
(212) 686-5522
Web site: http://www.unicefusa.org

UNICEF is an agency of the UN aimed at improving the health and education of mothers and their children in developing countries.

United Nations
3 United Nations Plaza
New York, NY 10017
(212) 963-8687
Web site: http://www.un.org
The UN is an international organization created in 1945 with the purpose of promoting international peace, security, and cooperation.

Web Sites

Due to the changing nature of Internet links, Rosen Publishing has developed an online list of Web sites related to the subject of this book. This site is updated regularly. Please use this link to access the list:

http://www.rosenlinks.com/itn/fail

For Further Reading

Adams, Simon. *The Role of the United Nations.* North Mankato, MN: Sea to Sea Publications, 2004.

Behnke, Alison. *Kim Jong-il's North Korea.* Breckenridge, CO: Twenty-First Century Books, 2007.

Connolly, Sean. *The United Nations.* Toronto, ON: Saunders Book Co., 2009.

Connolly, Sean. *UNICEF.* Toronto, ON: Saunders Book Co., 2009.

Delisle, Guy. *Pyongyang: A Journey in North Korea.* Montreal, QC: Drawn and Quarterly, 2005.

Donovan, Sandy. *Teens in Thailand.* Mankato, MN: Compass Point Books, 2009.

Downing, David. *War in Iraq.* Portsmouth, NH: Heinemann Library, 2005.

Grant, R. G. *NATO.* New York, NY: Franklin Watts, 2001.

Hussein, Ikram. *Teenage Refugees from Somalia Speak Out.* New York, NY: Rosen Publishing Group, 1997.

Langwith, Jacqueline. *Human Rights.* San Diego, CA: Greenhaven Press, 2007.

Lordan, Meredith. *The World Bank and the International Monetary Fund.* New York, NY: Chelsea House Publishers, 2008.

Moss, Carol. *Science in Ancient Mesopotamia.* New York, NY: Franklin Watts, 1998.

National Geographic and Mary Robinson. *Every Human Has Rights: What You Need to Know About Your Human Rights.* Des Moines, IA: National Geographic Children's Books, 2008.

Nelson, Sheila. *Decolonization: Dismantling Empires and Building Independence.* Broomall, PA: Mason Crest Publishers, 2006.

Reed, Jennifer Bond. *The Saudi Royal Family.* New York, NY: Chelsea House Publishers, 2002.

Sinkler, Adrian. *Saudi Arabia.* San Diego, CA: Greenhaven Press, 2003.

Smith, Roger. *UNICEF and Other Human Rights Efforts: Protecting Individuals.* Broomall, PA: Mason Crest Publishers, 2006.

Smithson, Ryan. *Ghosts of War: The True Story of a 19-Year-Old GI.* New York, NY: Collins, 2009.

Staples, Suzanne Fisher. *The House of Djinn.* New York, NY: Farrar, Straus and Giroux, 2008.

Williams, Mary E. *Human Rights: Opposing Viewpoints.* San Diego, CA: Greenhaven Press, 1998.

Yackley-Franken, Nicki. *Teens in Saudi Arabia.* Mankato, MN: Compass Point Books, 2007.

Bibliography

Ali, Ayaan Hirsi. *Infidel*. New York, NY: Free Press, 2008.

BBC News. "US Captain Rescued from Pirates." April 13, 2009. Retrieved August 13, 2009 (http://news.bbc.co.uk/2/hi/africa/7996087.stm).

CBC News. "UN Security Council Condemns North Korea Nuclear Test." May 25, 2009 Retrieved September 22, 2009 (http://www.cbc.ca/world/story/2009/05/25/north-korea-nuclear-test-reaction.html).

Engel, Richard. "Helping Iraqi Orphans." MSNBC, April 7, 2008. Retrieved September 1, 2009 (http://dailynightly.msnbc.msn.com/archive/2008/04/07/867267.aspx).

Fairclough, Gordon. "Tainting of Milk Is Open Secret in China." *Wall Street Journal*, November 3, 2008. Retrieved September 1, 2009 (http://online.wsj.com/article/SB122567367498791713.html?mod=google-news_wsj).

ForeignPolicy.com. "The 2009 Failed State Index." 2009. Retrieved September 1, 2009 (http://www.foreignpolicy.com//articles/2009/06/22/the_2009_failed_states_index).

Fund for Peace. "Welcome to the Fund for Peace." Retrieved September 2, 2009 (http://www.fundforpeace.org/web).

Ghani, Ashraf, and Clare Lockhart. *Fixing Failed States*. New York, NY: Oxford, 2008.

Goodspeed, Peter. "Mexico, Pakistan Face 'Rapid and Sudden' Collapse: Pentagon." *National Post*, January 15, 2009. Retrieved August 1, 2009 (http://www. nationalpost.com/news/world/story.html?id=1181621).

Hanson, Stephanie. "Backgrounder: Al-Shabaab." *New York Times*, March 2, 2009. Retrieved September 9, 2009 (http://www.nytimes.com/cfr/world/ slot2_20090227.html).

Hussain, Zahid. "Pakistan Taleban Take Over Towns as They Move Closer to Islamabad" Times Online, April 23, 2009. Retrieved September 9, 2009 (http://www.timesonline.co.uk/tol/news/world/asia/ article6150376.ece).

Karadsheh, Jomana. "Iraq Works to Reverse Doctor Brain Drain." CNN, September 29, 2008. Retrieved September 9, 2009 (http://www.cnn.com/2008/ WORLD/meast/09/29/iraq.doctors/index.html).

Krugman, Paul. "Erin Go Broke." *New York Times*, April 19, 2009. Retrieved September 9, 2009 (http://www. nytimes.com/2009/04/20/opinion/20krugman.html?_r=1).

Martin, Bradley K. *Under the Loving Care of the Fatherly Leader North Korea and the Kim Dynasty*. New York, NY: Thomas Dunne Books, 2004.

New York Times. "Text of the North Korean Announcement of Nuclear Test." May 24, 2009. Retrieved September 9,

2009 (http://www.nytimes.com/2009/05/25/world/asia/25nuke-text.html?_r=1).

New York Times. "Times Topics—Al-Shabab." 2009. Retrieved September 9, 2009 (http://topics.nytimes.com/top/reference/timestopics/organizations/s/al-shabab/index.html).

Parry, Richard Lloyd. "North Korea Is Fully Fledged Nuclear Power, Experts Agree." Times Online, April 24, 2009. Retrieved September 9, 2009 (http://www.timesonline.co.uk/tol/news/world/asia/article6155956.ece).

Perlez, Jane, and Pir Zubair Shah. "Taliban Exploit Class Rifts in Pakistan." *New York Times*, April 16, 2009. Retrieved September 9, 2009 (http://www.nytimes.com/2009/04/17/world/asia/17pstan.html).

Rohter, Larry. "The Crisis Came. Mexico Didn't Fail. Surprised?" *New York Times*, May 9, 2009. Retrieved September 9, 2009 (http://www.nytimes.com/2009/05/10/weekinreview/10rohter.html).

Sheridan, Michael. "Nation Under a Nuclear Coud." Times Online, October 15, 2006. Retrieved September 9, 2009 (http://www.timesonline.co.uk/tol/news/world/article600929.ece).

Index

About the Author

Matthew Bukovac is a writer who lives in New York City. He received a B.A. from SUNY Purchase and is a former Amnesty International student group organizer.

Photo Credits

Cover (top left) Scott Peterson/Getty Images; cover (top right) Khaled Desouki/AFP/Getty Images; cover (bottom) Farooq Naeem/AFP/Getty Images; pp. 4, 9 © AP Images; pp. 5, 46 Sipa Press/Newscom; pp. 11, 15 Wathiq Khuzale/Getty Images; p. 12 Fares Dlimi/AFP/Getty Images; p. 17 Tony Karumba/AFP/Getty Images; p. 18 Alexander Joe/AFP/Getty Images; p. 23 Paula Bronstein/Getty Images; p. 26 AFP/Getty Images; pp. 29, 34 Tariq Mahmood/AFP/Getty Images; p. 30 Alfred Eisenstaedt/Time & Life Pictures/Getty Images; p. 32 Getty Images; pp. 36, 42 Noah Seelam/AFP/Getty Images; p. 37 Business Wire via Getty Images; p. 38 Goh Chai Hin/AFP/Getty Images; pp. 45, 52 Pornchai Kittiwongsakul/AFP/Getty Images; p. 49 AFP/Newscom.

Designer: Tom Forget; Photo Researcher: Peter Tomlinson